I0441172

EXPERIENCES
OF A
SYSTEMIC COACH

ANTON DE KROON

Publisher: SystemicBooks
www.systemicbooks.com

ISBN 978-1537066479

Translation: James Campbell
Revision: Anton de Kroon

All rights reserved

Contents

1 Case studies **1**

1.1 Loyalty to the system of origin 1

1.2 Belonging and order 44

1.3 Propelling force 54

1.4 Systems confusion... 60

1.5 Other themes.. 67

2 Background **71**

2.1 Characteristics of systemic coaching.................... 72

2.2 Systemic-phenomenological basis....................... 75

2.3 My task 76

2.4 Awareness.. 77

2.5 Attitude... 78

2.6 What I often do.. 80

About the author: Anton de Kroon 85

About the (systemic) editor: James Campbell 86

Want to read a bit further?..................................... 87

Welcome

Welcome to my office to witness the coaching sessions I had with 25 people who came to me. Welcome to sit down beside me while I work as a systemic-phenomenological coach.

Both coachees and colleagues often asked me questions like: "Why do you say what you say?" "How do you come up with these, sometimes strange, but very touching comments?" At first, I replied that it just seems to go that way in my coaching conversations. But when I consider, analyse and reflect, there's clearly more to tell. In response, as an answer to those questions, I wrote this short book.

If this is your first encounter with systemic work, you should be aware that there is considerably more theory and background than I give here.

For each of the conversations I give the essence, interwoven with the feelings, thoughts or questions that arose in me. Each case ends with a brief reflection. Sometimes I explain why I made a certain choice, or shed some light on an issue or say what, in retrospect, I probably, or most certainly, could have done differently and better. Sometimes there are also valuable observations that emerged from feedback from colleagues with whom I looked back on a conversation or who read the draft.

Case studies form the core of this book and that's why they are in Part 1. Once I had written Part 1, I saw the need to add a second part, to provide a little more context and background and thus allow more insight.

Part 2 begins with the paragraph about systemic coaching from the book Systemic Consulting: The organisation as a living system (Authors: Siebke Kaat and Anton de Kroon). This is followed by a brief description of the systemic-phenomenological basis from which I work and, from that place, what I believe is my task as a coach. I continue by describing my awareness and attitude. Next you can read about some of the interventions that I frequently use when coaching. Finally, there is a short list of references and books about systemic-phenomenological work.

My wish is that reading this booklet inspires you to develop your own way of coaching and working, just as I have done from my conversations with coachees. By entrusting me with their questions – and themselves – they have made this possible.

Anton de Kroon
February 26, 2015
ak@hellingerinstituut.nl

1 Case studies

Gradually, throughout the conversations, I began to notice that there were certain returning themes. This led to me representing these themes via the following five subjects.

1.1 Loyalty to the system of origin

"Every time the same thing happens to me."

"I really want to change, but I just can't seem to."

Belonging to our system of origin (our family) sometimes leads to behaviour by which we unconsciously prove our loyalty to it and which, at the same time, causes us much suffering. If that's the case two things are entangled with each other that you can no longer, or not yet, separate: remaining loyal to your system of origin, and behaving in ways that once were good for you, but are no longer appropriate.

Often you find yourself repeating what someone else in your family did, behaviour that for them was appropriate. Or something that you picked up from that person. You just feel unable to do it differently, even though you really want to because it causes you trouble, sometimes a lot of trouble. But how?

It is possible to untangle this knot by inwardly saying to your father, mother, or others further back in the family line:

I love you, I'm grateful to you for life and everything else that I got from you. Until now I have done the things that I thought, unconsciously, were the only way to show that I love you. And there was a time when this behaviour was extremely helpful to me. I love you and will always love you, even when, starting now, I take my own path in life and do some things differently. So, please look kindly at me.

At the core, this is the movement that can bring change. Coachees are perfectly able to find their own ways, words or rituals that best fit them.
In one way or another, more than half of all the examples described concern this dynamic.

⚷ Up ... and ... down

We are in a workshop about taking a systemic look at money. For many participants it is interesting to discover how much their professional lives are influenced by the messages about money and power that they received as children. Messages which still show their effects in the fees that they do (or do not) dare to ask, how they do or do not build up reserves, how they deal with debtors and so on. What a big impact systemic loyalty has on our everyday behaviour. Besides the fact that money is money, what else can money represent in a system? How could you consciously choose your own way of dealing with money, rather than, unconsciously, be showing your love for your system of origin? This loyalty can manifest differently in different people.

Juliana's problem is that her earnings fluctuate widely: boom and bust. Sometimes she has plenty of work (and income) and then she's really broke. In response to what she says, I take the flipchart and draw a graph that goes up and down quite a few times. She nods agreement when I ask if it looks something like this.

The first question that comes to my mind is: "Did or does this phenomenon, of wildly-fluctuating income, occur with someone else in your family too?" After some pondering she shakes her head: "No."

Okay, I think, so it's not a *repeating pattern*. And while I am silent, because I don't know how to continue, Juliana says: "My parents have always been poor and still are." I draw a line along the bottom of the graph and say: "Is it true that, in their whole lives, your parents never rose above this line?" She nods affirmatively.

Then I tell her that children, totally unconsciously, sometimes make this promise: "I will not do better than you." And that this stems from loyalty to the system and a strong longing to belong to the system and the need of the system to exclude nobody.

On hearing this, Juliana goes quiet and says that for her there could be a lot of truth in what I say. And then, of course, she says: "Yes. So what now?"

What I explain to her, in brief, comes down to this: Say thank you to your parents for everything, really everything, that you got from them. Keeping all your love for them in your heart, tell them that you allow yourself to earn more than they have ever done and that your love for them remains just the same. You can also ask them to keep looking at you, their child, in a kind way, even if you become commercially successful.

0—ⲧ Reflection

I didn't give any attention to the emotional or financial significance of her problem or how she is dealing with it. If I had done that, it is likely that I would have been sucked into the problem from which - although I'm involved - I really need to take distance in order to see the whole. Of which this problem might be just one example.

It had never previously happened that I started drawing something on the basis of what the coachee is saying. At least until this conversation. I prefer to let people draw for themselves. It can already provide so much insight to see someone hesitating; see where they begin on the paper; what is drawn first; how the whole is built up and so on. And here, it is me who is drawing. It happened before I realised it. In retrospect, I think I was, perhaps, guided mostly by my own question: "Have I understood you correctly?" It was much less a question of: just draw what your problem looks like.

☛O To have or to be

We meet in Mexico City, just before he leaves for Chiapas, famous for its ancient Mayan culture. Marco is a sixty-year-old man with his own consulting firm. He calls his core business: *getting people moving*. He says his work has always had highs of doing well and lows of lack of money. With his hand he imitates the motion of a wave. Sometimes the lows were so deep that he had no money to buy food. His wife repeatedly threatened to divorce him if he was unable to provide a stable income. She's still there. She, too, seems to move with the fluctuations.

I say: "You said these highs and lows have been around a long time. Apparently, for one reason or another, they belong with you." And then Marco says: "Yes. It was the same with my father." Once, creditors demanded that he declare, under oath, that he had nothing left, even after they had already taken everything from him. He continues: "At an early age I read *To Have Or To Be* by Erich Fromm. That book had a tremendous affect on me. It seems for me it must be one or the other; its been that way my whole life."

I think what I see is loyalty to his father. How is it between him and his mother, I wonder. I ask him this question and he replies: "Without doubt to be represents my mother."

I tell him that children, even when they have become adults, remain connected to their parents and do things, not because they are good or useful, but because they want to show (unconsciously) their loyalty to the family system. And I ask him: "Could it perhaps be the case that when you're short of money you are loyal to your father, and when you're successful and happy you are loyal to your mother?" Marco's face turns pale, and in the silence that follows tears begin to flow. I continue: "Such is the love you have for each of your parents that you try to follow them both."

"I've never looked at it that way," he says, after a while.

I tell him he can let each of his parents know that he loves them and that he can ask both his father and his mother to look kindly at him as he goes his own way in life.

"Especially to my father," he says. "But how do I do that?" I also ask him to give the whole thing some time and to feel for himself how would best suit him to do this. Does he paint, does he sing, does he gather stones, does he write poetry? That's what I ask him. "You'll find your own way!"

Almost immediately, he says: "I know, I'm going to pray to my father." My last words: "Ah, maybe that's the reason you are going to Chiapas." He looks at me, dumbstruck and, in the embrace with which we say goodbye, I feel his tears on my cheek.

O━━☀ Reflection

Often I ask coachees to say when they first became aware of the problem they bring to our session. I do that to see if, in the past, something specific happened to which the problem might be a reaction. In this sense, a current problem might once have been a solution to a different problem; it might be a systemic reaction. When people say they cannot remember not having that problem, then it is not so much a particular event that triggered the problem but more a general state of being. And that could probably have to do with something very basic in the person or organisation, something that, out of systemic loyalty – so to say, has become one with that person or organisation.

When people can see what the systemic meaning of their problem might be, there are many who want to change instantly, and ask: "Okay, so what should I do now?"

I sketch a path they could possibly walk and then usually I leave it there, appealing to their own creativity to find a manner appropriate for them. A way that makes it their own.

⊶0 One pain that masks another

"I want my friend back." And then Cecilia says that she never manages to have a lasting relationship. Personally, I am impressed by the tremendous strength radiating from this young woman. And a thought arises in me: What kind of man is strong enough to make a place for himself, for Cecilia and also for a relationship with her? Men like that aren't easy to find!

My first question is: "What happened that made him leave?"

Then she says that their relationship was short, but also intense and full of potential. In the office building where they both work, one of her friends also works. He flirts a lot with her and also takes her out. Cecilia didn't like that and she said to him: "If you want to choose for her, then do so." He made his choice and now Cecilia is left with the consequences of what she said.

"His choice hurts you," I say. Her response: "I feel pain in my heart, and this is not the first time." My response: "That pain does not come through to me in the words you said to him; and what you did say sounds so reasoned and detached."

She understands my comment but indicates that she does not know how she could have put it differently. I try to explain but she cannot take it in. So I switch: "Imagine that the two of us are in a relationship. However, there is another man whom you also find interesting and attractive. And then I say to you: If you prefer to go with him, then go."

I ask her what she feels when I say that to her. "I feel rejected." "Right! It's like telling him that you don't care if he chooses the other woman. And how does it feel for you when I say: "It hurts my heart when you go with her; stay with me." "Yes, of course, it should hurt," was her response. And: "That's why it goes wrong every time. I speak from my mind and not from my heart."

So strange, I think to myself, that such a powerful, intelligent woman can spoil it for herself this way, every time. But somehow, obviously, there's a very good reason for it. "What are you trying to protect when you torture yourself like this?" "My mother ... I think," she answers spontaneously. Her mother seems to have had a hard life, which could be said for Cecilia too. "I want to take her pain away."

"You love your mother so much!" Then I talk to her about how separating her love for her mother from her relationship behaviour could bring the changes and relationship she so desires.

0━━🗝 Reflection

I do not go into emotions; into how sad and painful this issue is for Cecilia. If I do that I obstruct both my own and her path towards the systemic content. So, immediately, I question her for facts: What happened? And as I ask that question, another one is in the back of my mind: Could this 'something' have happened more often? And if that were the case, for what is this recurring pattern a good solution? Or in other words: What, systemically, still needs to be put in place so that this pattern is no longer necessary?

I use my own awareness to clarify what her comments bring up in me. This helps her to see her blind spots.

It is curious that this intelligent and socially-adept woman simply cannot and 'will' not understand what effect her business-like words had on her boyfriend. For me the question is: What is so precious and fragile that it must be protected by being *not understood*?

The question of what she is trying to protect arises in me because I ask myself the question: If you torment yourself, from what does that distract you, so that you focus not on the real cause but on the self-inflicted pain? Like when you pinch your arm really hard if you've banged your toe. The self-inflicted pain in your arm distracts you from the pain in your toe.

I'm sharing this coaching experience with a colleague and she says: "It looks to me as if you, as the coach, had not withdrawn far enough from the mother-daughter system. It would have been worth investigating whether the daughter's loyalty to the larger family system is the deeper reason for what she unconsciously does. To whom or to what is she being loyal when she wishes to remove her mother's heavy burden? Could there be a connection between her intellectual way of communicating and a desire to protect her mother?" Valuable ideas to remember for the next time.

⊢——O "I can't do two things at once."

Miriam is an accountant and is participating in a Systemic Interventions learning group. The work really resonates with her, but one way or another, in her work as an accountant, she fails to do anything with what she learns here. She wants to talk about it.

"I can't do two things at once," is how she begins to sketch out her situation. One way or another it sounds to me like a learned phrase. So I rephrase it as a message from someone else: "You cannot do two things at once!" And, looking for the source: "From whom did you first hear this?" Instantly, she says her mother. When I ask how old she was when she heard that for the first time, she says: "I only know that it has always been said to me like that."

I respond very enthusiastically to her words: "Right. You do not know any better! How, then, would you ever be able to do two things at once? That's just not possible. And, once, it was a fantastic solution for something, and you have really got a lot out of proving that you cannot do two things at once."

"In some way, for your mother, this has been an important and loving message, which she gave to you in order to be of service to you. We do not need to know the background. What can happen, therefore, is that you, as an affectionate and loving child, behaved and still behave in accord with that message. At some point you have made it so much your own that you cannot do otherwise. Up till now, besides the fact that you can now feel the limitations of the message, it has also brought you something very good, for which you can be grateful."

It is really impossible for her to imagine what that 'something very good' could have been. And yet, systemically, acknowledging that, is the only way for her to be able to behave differently. My focus is on the movement of including, of being grateful for what it has brought, and then of letting go.

So I say to Miriam: "It could well have been to ensure that you became a nice person, absolutely not arrogant, not someone who beats her own drum shouting 'Look at what I can do'. Making yourself bigger than you are." She responds by saying that she feels rather modest. And I become even more enthusiastic: "Exactly! That's a great quality of yours. And that could well be a direct result of the message that you cannot do two things at once. If you can be grateful for this outcome, then the message has achieved its goal and you can begin experimenting, modestly, with doing two things at once. And then, perhaps three, and so on. The risk that this will make you a terribly arrogant person seems extremely remote."

Satisfied, she gets up from the seat next to me and leaves.

O──ᴛ Reflection

A 45-year old woman, an accountant, who can't do two things at once. That is strange. Instead of going into how it is for her, what is annoying and so on, I reflect on the fact that I find it curious. A worthwhile curiosity. I do not judge it.

When did that start and for what was it, at that time, a good solution, I wonder. And then the idea comes up: she doesn't create this concept herself, it must have been said by someone else and then have been internalised. And then I go to the source only, and not to every single occasion when it was confirmed that she cannot do two things at once.

What motivated her mother is unimportant to me. There's no doubt that her mother had good reason to do what she did. The only thing that matters to me is the fact that her mother gave the message and Miriam accepted it.

For many people being grateful for the good in your life, that came from behaviour you no longer want, is a totally new perspective.

The same colleague from the previous case has a more profound question: What happened in the family system when doing two things at once, that had consequences so disastrous that it became such an important message? Another beautiful question to remember.

⊶ "With us, nothing is what it seems."

Word-of-mouth brought Carola to me. She works as an HR manager in a large factory and has recently been asked to take on a different HR role at another location. "I haven't done that kind of work but, of course, I can learn it!" she recalls saying. She agreed to the move, but felt unhappy and did not know what to do about this. I notice the thought that she agreed rather too quickly and is just taking the consequences for granted.

"It's all misty," she says, and continues with a story which brings me also into mist. I tell her that the same thing has come over me: mist! In an attempt to break the impasse, I ask her to draw the mist. She looks at me, a bit unsettled, but I push a pencil and paper into her hand. I respond to her questioning look with: "Where are you in the mist?" She draws a big question mark on the paper. Gradually come crosses and balloons that, for her, represent various elements.

The core of the story is that she took a position that was intended for someone else, and that person was also transferred to another location. My first question asks whether this happens more often in this company. Then it would, indeed, be strange if it was happening differently now. She doesn't recognise that, so I decide to look at her own life: "Do you recognise yourself as often being in places or situations where you don't want to be? Think of the past." Then she says, that as the eldest of two children, she always had to do things that her sister refused to do, because her sister wanted to do something else.

⚿ Reflection

Events like that easily make someone into a person who constantly does what the outside world wants, without fulfilling her own desires or needs. Once you are like that, how could you ever change! Whatever you do, you feel unhappy.

Usually, for a small child, such behaviour ensures the appreciation of their parents. And as a child that makes you happy; it makes you belong. Once you are an adult you feel, unconsciously, a sense of betrayal when you try to stop this familiar behaviour. Mostly though, you also just don't know how you could do it differently, even though it makes you really unhappy.

I also explain to Carola how, if she wants to, she *could* do it differently. (As I have already described in the introduction to this section.)

In parting, I ask her what the company where she works produces. "With us, nothing is what it appears to be. We make plastic parts for cars, which look as if they are made of metal." I let something slip out: "Oh, that seems a bit like how it is with you . . . " Laughing together, we say goodbye.

A few days later we bump into each other at a conference. She wants to talk to me. "I've been thinking a lot about what you said, but I find it so hard to say <u>No</u>. Can you help me with that?" At my request, she accompanies me to an empty room. First of all, I ask her if she will swap her statement that she *finds it so hard to say No* for *I'm not so used to saying Yes to myself*. When that has landed in her, and she nods, I ask her to stand opposite me, about one and a half meters away.

I have a pen in my hand and I say: "This pen represents an instruction from me to you. One that you do not want to do." Then I move the hand with the pen closer to her. While the pen is still closer to me than to her, she reaches out her hand to take the pen. "You're incredibly eager to take it," I say. "If I were your boss, I would find it very difficult not to use your eagerness, especially if it would benefit me. Let's try something else. Stand with your hands behind your back and feel what happens if I try to give the pen to you." When I insist that she takes the pen, it is almost impossible for her to hold that stance: she turns deathly pale. Then I ask her to step slowly backwards, further and further away, and feel what this brings up in her. Her normal complexion returns, her breathing becomes calmer. "It's easier here," she says.

I conclude by saying: "Literally 'taking distance' seems to help you to make your own choices." She agrees. "Well, now you know what to do."

0━━⚷ Reflection

If I lose my way in someone's story, then the first question I ask myself is: Does what is happening in the coachee or her story also echo in me? Instead of going into the content by asking clarifying questions, I often stop the dialogue, in the firm belief that more of the same will not help us.

Words will not help Carola or me to find a path through the mist. So I stop, abruptly, and switch to another mode of expression, making a drawing; I insist that she must draw!

In retrospect, I wonder if I am just too quick in wanting to solve the problem of the mist, in order to see what is 'really' going on. "Have I welcomed the mist? What might be better left shrouded in mystery? Who would be scared to death if the veil suddenly dissolved? What would be painful or dangerous to see?"

If a person has a problem in an organisation, then for me the question is always where the problem sits. Mainly with the organisation or mainly with the person? If I am to know which way I need to go, a crucial question is if this issue or behaviour occurs frequently in the business where the person works. Which, in this case, seemed to be a dead end; so I turned the other way, to her own life. And, indeed, it was more common there.

When, with the pen, we practise refusing any assignments that she does not want, I think it's important to get to the source of the behaviour, rather than the behaviour itself. And the source deserves a positive label. Do not say: "You should not do it," but, "Wow, you really are prepared to do it!"

I repeat to her what the effects appear to be of what she has been doing, in order to reaffirm what, at that moment, simply is. And afterwards I think, rather paternalistically, there is the risk that I make her smaller and, thus, myself bigger.

When a colleague reads the draft of this text he notes: "When you went to work with that pen, you could also have stayed on the systemic track by examining whether she, perhaps, is performing the tasks of someone else in her system by doing what she does." Yes, that would have been worth doing, and might have led to a solution at a deeper level. A step in that direction could be made with questions such as: Who would be happy if you would do it differently? And: Who would be upset or disappointed seeing you do that?

⌐─⟨🎸⟩ Meeting with an interpreter

I cannot resist looking and investigating systemically - and never want to - so I got talking to the interpreter who was translating from English to Spanish during a workshop. I told her that I think it's special work, making it possible for two parts of a system to understand each other. These parts would have nothing to do with each other if she, or at least her function, would not be there.

"How did you come to be an interpreter?" Then she tells me that she first studied psychology, but eventually chose to study languages as she liked this more. In addition to her native language - Spanish - she also studied German and English, attaining fluency through studying in Germany and England respectively. She feels as if she just, somehow, fell into this work.

Systemically, this didn't help me at all. A thought arose: when a child occupies a place in the birth order, for example the middle – which could entail much mediation with the other children - then, as an interpreter, you might be continuing to fulfil this function.

"If there were several children in your family of origin, what was your place in the line of children?" I noticed I was slightly disappointed to learn she was the oldest. However, it quickly became obvious that I was on the right track, but I had filled-in too much. This became clear when, without prompting, she continued: "Within a year of my birth my brother arrived and, seven years later, a sister. And it is really funny that my parents needed me in order to understand my brother.

When he began to babble, I always knew exactly what he meant and quite often I had to explain that to my parents. They understood nothing that he said!"

"To me it looks as if you are able to bring that special quality to your profession: making it possible for people to understand each other."

✂━ Reflection

During the training, I was impressed by how powerfully and focused this interpreter worked to achieve her goal: that all the participants understand each other. During the final dinner we found ourselves talking about relationships and she said, to her dismay, this element was missing in her life.

As a I write, this question arises: Might one call the unconscious force that drives her life being between? And if your quality is to be between, what do you have to do to really be with someone? How do you make that happen for each other? And at what price? Afterwards, a colleague chips in with a nice theme, raising the question of whether the pattern started with her or whether it already existed and came to her from the system.

A very different point: that a good interpreter works for the whole seems obvious, but it's also a very lonely place from which they contribute to the whole. I feel fresh inspiration for how I might thank an interpreter in a future workshop.

⌫═══O "I want to break a pattern I have with my mother."

Especially in the beginning, I don't need to know what the pattern is. So the first question I ask Maria is: "Since when has the pattern been there?" It seems to have started when she was around thirty. Looking at her I guess that was at least twenty-five years ago. And of course my next question is: "What happened at that time?" "My brother committed suicide."

"And what has that to do with the pattern between you and your mother?" "My mother is guilty of my brother's suicide. I really blame her."

"You love your brother very much," is my first reaction. With that I go to the source of the connection from which her reproach and exclusion originate. "You desperately want him back, alive." Her reaction is unmistakable: I've hit the nail on the head.

We are in a very Catholic country – and I know Catholicism well, from earlier in my own life. That gives me an idea: "I want to say something very strange to you. May I?" Although she gives me a startled look, she nods in agreement. "In relation to your mom, with your judgment of her, you are taking the place of God. Since you're clearly not God, you have no right to take that place!" And after a pause: "Come back to your right place as a daughter in a relationship with her mother."

After a silence, I ask her if she knows – if that's what she would like – how she can do that. She shakes her head: "No". With her permission I am ready to tell her how she can, but first I want to say something else.

"Both your mother and your brother did what each of them, at that moment, believed was best. Both had their own reasons and backgrounds. It's horrible for you to miss your brother, but this is a separate matter. What happened is just what happened. That's all. And, from that point onwards, everyone has to go on living with this fact and bearing the pain. Judgements about this are inappropriate and will not help you any further. If you judge your mother – no matter how understandable that is, given the pain you feel due to the death of your brother – then you place yourself, as the child, above your mother, and that weakens both you and your relationship with your mother."

I suggest that we do a little exercise (and it went at a much slower pace than described here). "Imagine your mother, position yourself opposite her, look at her and say: You are my mother, I am your daughter; I owe my life to you. Your son, who is also my brother, is no longer here. Just as you have your pain because of this, I too have my pain." And I close with: "See if you, in your own way, can make an honest bow to your mother."

⊙━━ᵐᵐ Reflection

I am again and again surprised and pleased at how quickly just two questions can bring you to the core issue: "Since when?" and "What happened then?" Then the problem is on the table, although not yet solved, but still . . .

I also have a brother who put an end to his life. Instantly, my pain is touched by hearing her story. For a moment I have the urge to tell her, but realise that it's not appropriate; it has no function for her. So I don't.

Sometimes, as in this case, and if people do not fully understand this work, I give a short lecture about looking and acting systemically. Then a little bit of explaining is appropriate.

Sometimes I feel like playing with the order of the two sentences: "You are my mother," and, "I am your daughter." Do you start with recognising the place of the other and then you take your place, or vice-versa? In this example, where Maria placed herself above her mother, I chose for her: first to recognize the place of her mother and secondly her own place. Then the order is correct again.

☞ "I always spoil everything."

Paula looks a smart, energetic woman. Someone you could trust to get on with things! It is evident that in the Systemic Intervention training in which she participates, I talk a lot about patterns, because she came straight to the point: "I'm trapped in a constant pattern where I just end up feeling unhappy. And yet I cannot stop myself. "

It's nice that a coachee already formulates her question so systemically.

When I ask her what the pattern consists of, what it is she does, she says: "In my work and in my relationships I lash-out so wildly at everything around me that nothing remains. I've had wonderful jobs: in my last job they offered to pay me twice as much if I stayed; I didn't. If a nice man appears in my life, it doesn't take long before I quarrel so much that he leaves."

"There's a power in the way you talk about what you do to yourself, rather than blaming others for what they do to you. I guess what you do produces quite a bit of misery for you." Half laughing and half reproachfully she looks at me and says: "I cannot imagine for what this could be a solution!"

Here she's referring to a phrase I often use during training courses: problems are solutions. With that I indicate that, at the level of the individual or organisation, something can be a problem and at the same time – at the systemic level – both a signal and a solution.

The question, for what might a particular problem be the solution, is perhaps not so easy for clients and students to answer. It needs practice in this way of seeing and thinking. Keeping the same intention, the question can be formulated quite differently, in such a way that it strikes a chord in the person you ask.

That is why I continue with: "Maybe I'm asking the impossible of you, but imagine this whole pattern of yours would disappear, that you'd never behave that way again, what would you miss terribly?" I believe less than two seconds passed between my last and her first word.

"The care and attention of my parents." She startles herself and starts to cry, a bit carefully because she doesn't want her mascara to run.

"And their care and attention is so important to you that you do many things, unconsciously, in order to ensure you screw up. People can be extraordinarily complex, don't you think?" She sighs a yes.

"Needing care and attention makes me think of a small child. At your age it is nice to feel the love of your parents; care and attention you no longer need. And for a long time, apparently, given your behaviour, it has been important for you to invite your parents to continue treating you as a child."

Her response: "Stupid eh!" Then mine: "On the contrary, I think it's smart, because it works very well. You get what you want." And now, as a grown-up woman, with a bit more insight into what is really happening in the way you act, do you have an idea what you could do to change it? If you really want that."

And after we look, peacefully, at each other, she sighs and nods. My response: "Beautiful. Is this enough for now?" Thoughtfully, with moist eyes, she nods yes.

━● Reflection

Elsewhere I write that I usually have no interest in knowing the pattern someone is talking about. I am much more interested in the fact that the pattern exists and knowing what good that (now cursed) pattern ever yielded. In this case, however, I did ask, and I do not know why. I did it intuitively. What it brings up in me is that I can honestly say that with this pattern, she causes herself a lot of misery. But I do not go into the pattern: what she does; what happens then; how that makes her feel and so on, because that would divert me from the systemic path.

In retrospect I think that when I asked her to look at whatever her behaviour might be a good solution for, I could have chosen a different direction. In doing what she does, is she taking on the role of someone else in her system? During the coaching session this never occurred to me. A question in that direction could be: Who else screwed it up for themselves? Or, who would be very happy if you change this pattern? And, who will be happy if you continue with it? How do your parents and grandparents look at you? All this from the fact that loyalty to the family system can lead to one family member unconsciously continuing the unfinished business of an earlier family member.

➤ Did you grow up in an orphanage?

Maria wants to talk about a problem with her work. She is a middle-aged woman and says she has worked her entire life as a freelancer; first here, then there, then somewhere else. She is fed up with it; she would like to have a permanent job. At the same time the idea makes her feel insecure.

My first question: "What's attractive about the way you've worked up till now?" Then she talks about being free and without ties. When I ask what she would like most of all, she says: "I would also like to really belong somewhere."

A question arises in me: Where else did you not really belong? And then a question slips out of my mouth: "Did you grow up in an orphanage?" She replies: "No. Just at home, with my parents."

She wants to know why I asked such a weird question. I talk about unconscious loyalty to the system of origin and repeating patterns as an expression of that loyalty. And applying this lens to her, led me to look for the field where she, as a child, possibly didn't belong. And then the question about the orphanage spontaneously burst out of me. And now I am silent. Maria is also silent. After a while she turns to me and says: "My father was in an orphanage." It turns out that we both get goose bumps. "Yes, and what now?" she asks.

As previously described, I explain how she can maintain her love for her father without being the same as him: never belonging anywhere.

🔑 Reflection

If people want to get rid of something, systemically seen this is a movement of exclusion. The system resists this movement because it has a basic need to acknowledge everything that belongs. So my first movement with coachees is to start looking for the good that their behaviour has brought them up till now. Not in order to leave things as they are, but rather to make change possible. If there is sincere recognition and gratitude for the good that a certain behaviour has brought, this allows you to find a new way. You could, for example, say a phrase like: "Thank you for what you have brought me so far, and now the time has come for me to do it differently." Here I think it is crucial that and is said and not but. Using but would repeat the excluding movement and would negate the earlier "thank you".

Once, in Maria's unconscious, it was important to choose a way of being that connected her with her father: both of them not really belonging. It is about facing up to that. And being proud and grateful towards yourself that, for a time, you did it that way. And then to give a place to the realization that you can do it differently now, without giving up your love for your father or taking distance from it.

➤ "I've been trying to do it my whole life."

Teresita is a woman of 65 who, as soon as she sits next to me, with moist eyes, says: "My whole life I've been trying to untangle a knot and I haven't managed to." I wait till her tears stop and her breathing becomes calmer. I say, "I've a strange observation. May I tell you it? " She nods. "If you have been trying, for so long, without success, to untangle the knot, perhaps it is not intended that you succeed."

She looks at me like I'm from another planet. And that is also true, a bit; from the 'planet' systemic perception. Her confusion is visible and palpable. I add a little more: "Maybe that knot is not only from and for you, but from and for someone else in your family of origin. Your mother perhaps, or grandmother, or even further back." She says: "I almost cannot believe it's not my job to solve it." I respond: "Perhaps it is indeed from and for you, but also perhaps not."

She agrees with my proposal to do a meditation with her. I suggest she holds her arms slightly away from her body, hands open as if to accept something. I ask her to take in one hand It's my job and in the other hand It's not my job. I ask her to say Yes, as much to one as to the other, and to feel how heavy or light each weighs, or whether anything changes in hand or arm; what happens if she moves her hand and so on. At one point I ask her - without thinking about it - to feel if her arms or hands want to do something or be moved by a force outside of her – and to allow that. Very slowly, searching as it were, she brings her hands together, as if both options are included.

"What a special experience," she says afterwards. "And what do I do now?" My response: "For the moment, nothing. For a few minutes you have been looking, in a different way, at something that you've devoted your whole life to seeing in one particular way. Give yourself some time to get used to the idea that maybe it's not your job. It really seems as if, until now, the job had you in its grip. Maybe you will grip the job now in your hands and that will give other options." She agrees to leave it at that.

⚷ Reflection

If something is not working, the question is what is the systemic message. Should you keep doing your best and trying new approaches or face the fact that 'never succeeding' actually is a gift. In the latter case, you can determine whether you are trying to accomplish someone else's task – which is why you don't succeed – or whether it's important for you to stop trying and by accepting that, to learn from it.

I choose a meditation in which I ask, literally, that at the same time she takes both possibilities in her hands, in order to break the impasse: the impasse that only one thing is possible. For me it means being open to find out whatever could be possible and letting her body experience what happens.

▬O Step by step

Annemarie is the mother of a one-year-old girl and has a business together with her husband. She says that she feels unhappy because she spends too little time with her daughter: "I want to give her more time and attention, but I don't manage to." She continues, saying that she does exactly the same as her mother did to her, and as her grandmother did with her daughter: frequent and long absences because of work. And she had already resolved to do it better if she had a child . . .

I tell her I see her behaviour as an extraordinary expression of love for her mother and her family, and its message is 'I'm just like you; with what I do I prove that I belong with you.' And that's a very good reason to get yourself in a real muddle about the choice between child and work.

"Perhaps I can see it like that, but what can I do with it!" A logical comment for a woman like Annemarie, who also loves to hurry. Previously, under the heading Loyal to the system of origin, I described the process that helps someone to do both the one thing (to remain faithful to the family) and the other (to behave differently). I explain that to her.

Of course, coachees focus on their own problems. In the end, that's what troubles them. And of course they put out a request for help because they – despite attempts to do so – have not yet been able to resolve it themselves. With sincere respect for how the coachee sees the problem, I try to direct her focus towards the solution.

She says she has no idea how she could do it differently – the distribution of attention and energy between child and work. She agrees to do a guided meditation, as follows (very briefly): Imagine you go to bed after a typical day and, after tossing and turning about the fact that today again you gave too little attention to your daughter, eventually you fall asleep. A peaceful and deep sleep. And, while sleeping, it happens: the miracle that, when you wake up in the morning, you know exactly how, from then on, you are going to give optimal attention and love to your daughter. Your life has become just the way you want it. You wake up, get up and notice how totally different your life is.

Tears stream down her cheeks. After a while I ask her if she knows how to take a first step. "I'm so scared," she says. I ask her to take her fear very seriously.

I put my right hand up at the right side of my body, palm facing her, and tell her that this hand stands for all her fears. I invite her to look at the fear. In the beginning her eyes shoot back and forth between my hand and my eyes. Slowly she focuses more on the hand and her breathing becomes calmer. In answer to my question if the fear might also be telling her something, she nods: "It says it is not so big and it is not that bad."

Then I hold my left hand up to the left side of my body and tell her that this hand represents how, exactly like after the miracle, she will go forward with her daughter and work. She looks for a long time at my left hand. I invite her to look again at the fear. When she does, a slight smile appears on her face. And back to the other hand. She nods when I ask her, after a while, if she has seen enough.

Showing the way to anyone who asks for it, is how I see my job as a coach. And once somebody has seen the new path, they can take it again themselves at the time and in the manner that best suits them. So I ask her now how far along we are. She says: "I'm not sure if it's the right direction." My response: "No, of course you're not." I ask her to stand up and, in her mind's eye, to choose the direction in which she would like to take her first step. Once she has chosen, I ask her to slowly take a few steps in that direction. Then I stop her and say, "You thought you were on the right path, but now you're here you come to the conclusion that this is not the case. What do you do?" Spontaneously she chooses another direction and takes a few steps . . .

I wish her much good fortune on this voyage of discovery, as her body language and words show that we are finished.

⚷ Reflection

Everything that is, is there for a reason. That leads me to keep on saying yes to whatever exists, to all that is. Not chipping away at it, asking if it could, perhaps, be a little less. In a mini-constellation I bring the anxiety into the here and now.

When one problem is 'solved' Annemarie comes with another one. She does this a few times. Each subsequent issue I take very seriously and each is just as welcome to me. In that respect, during the session I went along with her and, each time, took each new step with her.

That felt right, at that moment. But was every step really that new? Or did I just repeat her pattern with her? Would it have helped her more to have asked if she perhaps had unconsciously taken on the task of someone else in her system. For example I could have asked: Who in your family also suffered from terrible fear? Who in your family was also uncertain whether they would go in the right direction?

One of the basic needs for a system to survive is that it needs to be complete, that there is a place for all the parts that belong to it. Systemic forces cause parts of the whole - without them being aware of it - to collaborate in keeping it complete. Another term that is sometimes used is that you – unconsciously – are taken into service by the system. In this case that could, for example, mean that Annemarie unconsciously carries out the system's command not to exclude her mother and grandmother, thus keeping the system complete. She could do this by, for example, acting in the same way with her child as the women before her in the family system. Being loyal to the system, doing what it asks of you without being aware of it, can carry a high price: being deeply unhappy about how you raise your own child. And then the two loyalties are in conflict with each other: personal, conscious loyalty (I want to be there for my child) and systemic, unconscious loyalty (I will do it just like you and I will not be there enough for my child). No wonder you cannot find a way through this. If this is how it was in Annemarie's life, that conflict of loyalties has been kept out of the picture.

☞ "Yes, it's my loyalty!"

Patricia is a participant in a Systemic Interventions training. The moment she comes into the room my attention is drawn to a piece of jewellery she is wearing. It fits rather tightly around her neck, made of thick double links. Although a somewhat elegant design, it still looks heavy, very heavy. The chain I use to lock up my bike is, of course, quite different, but that's what her jewellery reminds me of. Unusual, I think to myself.
At the end of the second day, she wants to talk to me.

During the training it had already become clear that Patricia usually converses in an almost unstoppable stream of words. In our conversation, I often had to interrupt her as she wanted to give more and more examples and details.

She says she had worked for years, with great pleasure, in a high-level management job at a car manufacturer. What she especially enjoyed were meetings they sometimes had with a large group of women in similar positions. And suddenly there came, as she calls it, a 'male policy' and she had to leave. Then began a period of eight years during which she repeatedly started her own businesses, sometimes alone, once with one of her sons and once together with her husband. And everything she has done since leaving the car factory has cost her too much energy. "How on earth do I put a stop to this?"

I ask if I may tell her what I've noticed, and that perhaps it might not make sense. I say that her necklace brings to mind the words heavy and chained. "To what are you chained or, conversely, what has chained itself to you?" While I'm speaking I get a picture of a cartoon: someone in prisoner clothes with a ball-and-chain around his ankle; someone who takes a step with his free leg, then has to stop because of the weight he's dragging, before pulling the other leg along. While telling her this, I get up from my chair and take a couple of 'dragging' steps forward. I say, "That's how it looks to me. Does that resonate with you or is it nonsense?" She goes very pale and says nothing. That last thing, in particular, is rather unusual.

Then she nods and says, "Yes, that's how it feels." After a while I ask her if she has any idea what the heavy ball represents. She nods and says that the ball stands for her loyalty.

We are quiet for a moment and then I ask her: "How would it be if you removed the necklace for a while, that you free yourself from it?" Instantly, she starts to open the clasp. "Hey! Not so fast. Take some time to consider what you are doing." Her response was: "No, it's got to come off." And so it did and she stuffed the necklace in her purse. Moments later, she says: "I know enough."

⌐⊕ Reflection

Open observations, without prejudice, create possibilities for me as a coach. So, from the first moment, the jewellery is playing a role. It is doing something to me.

Asking if I may say something strange has never ever evoked a rejection. It is a sign that I'm going in another direction than (I think) people expect me to. It focuses their attention.

It might also happen that, at the very start, I ask a coachee who has very high expectations: "Are you willing to take the risk that maybe I can't do anything for you?" Nobody has ever quit following that question. For me, it is an important element of the contract that stops me trying to solve the problem of the coachee, but to let it stay as his problem. Incidentally, it also helps when I ask myself: What is special, that would be lost if the coachee really solved his problem? In other words: What is it that makes it very valuable for the coachee – at the systemic level – to have this problem rather than to solve it?

Later, I was evaluating this session with a colleague who sketched a beautiful systemic possibility: Does it, perhaps, concern loyalty to a family member who once was in chains, who was, or maybe still is, in prison?

⚊○ "I want a partner."

Ana asks for an interview and, to help you make sense of her initial observations, I first want to say something about a previous coaching session in the learning group.

During a group session a woman discovered that in her quest for a life partner she was actually looking for her father. So new relationships went wrong because she hadn't yet found a man who also wanted to be her father. During the coaching session I had explained how she could take her father back as her father, accept the pain of missing him and so set herself free for a possible future partner.

Ana sits down next to me and says: "I think I do that too, look for my father in a new partner". I say: "That could be; it occurs more often. What is your question?"

Then she says she divorced seven years ago. Because we're speaking in our own mix of English and Spanish – I'm handicapped in Spanish, she's limited in English – it is unclear to me who initiated the divorce. For me it makes quite a difference which place you occupy in the process. Are you the instigator or are you the one it happens to? And does that pattern
suit you? It turns out that it was Ana who started divorce proceedings.

"I'd like a new relationship but they never work out. I don't want to go out on the hunt for a man, but I do want a nice relationship."

I ask her if the place next to her is available. She closes her eyes, takes a moment to turn her face towards me, opens her eyes and says: "No." And after a while: "I know enough."

⚷ Reflection

Here I thought it was important to ask, "What's your question?" to shift the focus from the previous coachee to Ana herself. In general, when in a potential stream of words and examples from a coachee, I'm quickly minded to ask: "What's your question?" Where does the coachee want to end up? Meaning: in what is he probably entangled, and what is his ultimate goal.

Also during the session, I can sometimes come back with "What's your question now?" Or: "How far along are you with finding an answer to your question?" It focuses the coachee towards a solution and it avoids me going to work to find my answer to her question.

I had, earlier, deliberately chosen not to go into the relationship with her father. She had discovered enough about that in another participant's session.

Many of the changes that people want are focussed on the future. That longing keeps people busy. Systemically, however, what comes first is the question of whether the past is ready to let the future emerge. Or does that past need something else before it unlocks the door to the future? Often it needs recognition of what it has contributed to how things are now. Even though the way it is now is exactly what you want to get away from. Precisely by giving recognition and thanks to the past, everyone who wants to go towards the future is then allowed to do so.

⚯— "I'm so scared."

Two days later, Ana asks once again if she can talk to me. This time about her son. "I'm afraid something will happen to him. I dream that he gets seriously injured or commits suicide. Sometimes I'm terribly afraid that really will happen!"

"Yes, like to any human being, something fatal could happen to him. For you, as his mother, that would of course be a disaster. That fear is yours, you should not load it onto him. He has his own problems and should make the best of dealing with them himself." It seems like a sort of revelation for Ana: "Oh. That helps. It is my fear. I must keep it to myself!"

And then she tells a bit more. The boy turns out to be 17 years old and hasn't been going to school for a few years. That can go unnoticed and unpunished in the country where they live. Her son spends a lot of time in his room constantly busy at the computer. "He doesn't just play games, he also looks at everything; he is interested in the news and knows a lot. But he's very withdrawn."

In answer to my question about when this started, Ana says that it began around the time she and her husband separated, seven years ago. When I ask about the nature of the contact between her son and his father, she says that it had been bad for a long time, but now is going much better. Sometimes they go to the movies together.

She continues: "My son is very nice to me, sometimes he just gives me a kiss and says he loves me. But I can be so scared. Recently I was at a hamburger bar with him and we were waiting for our order. Suddenly I couldn't see him anywhere.

Then terror strikes my heart." She shows me how she, hardly

able to breathe, wide-eyed, looks twice, rapidly, to the left and right. This is not how you look for your seventeen year old son, but for a child of two or three, I think to myself, and I say this to Ana. "Yes, that's right," she says. I continue: "He is seventeen years old. But if you think about him right now, how old is he to you? "Twelve," she says.

"Okay; imagine your son is in front of you; in your mind let him grow from twelve to seventeen years old." She first looks at a point on the ground three meters away, then she raises her head and looks straight ahead. After a while she says: "He's not a kid anymore." I confirm this: "He is now a young adult."

"It seems I'm repeating what my mother did to me. I had an almost symbiotic relationship with her. She was always grabbing me around my belly and pulling me onto her lap; very protective!" Ana has already experienced, a few times in the training group, me explaining to someone how you can let go of repeating what a parent did, while maintaining the love from which the behaviour comes. So I limit myself to: "You know how to handle it." She nods.

I wonder how she would deal with any other children; would the same pattern manifest? Therefore, I ask her if she has more children. For a moment I think I see her hesitate before she says that there are three. I tell her that to me she seemed to hesitate. "That's right," she says. "I have three living children, two daughters and a son. One, though, a boy, died in my womb."
"So you have four children. Or perhaps even more?" This appears not to be the case. When I ask whether the deceased child in some way has a place in her home, she says his name and that she has candles for all four children.

"Nice that you also give your dead child a place in your life. Could it be that the love and care you have for your still-born child is carried over a bit onto your other, living son? Perhaps afraid to lose him too?" Then she really has to cry.

When she calms down, I ask her to put both hands one behind the other, palms facing her, so she can see only one hand. I tell her each hand represents one of her boys. I ask her to move each of her hands slowly sideways, left to left and right to right. I ask her to stop only when the hands are far apart, and then to look a few times alternately to one and then to the other. I say it will become clear which son is represented by which hand. She nods vigorously.

After a while I say: "It could just be that, unconsciously, you have merged your boys, as it were. And the loss that you had once, you do not want again. Very understandable."

Ana says: "I have to keep them apart and not to load them with the weight of my fears and worries." In this one sentence she formulated exactly what her task is. I added that, in her thoughts, she can go with her fears and concerns to her mother who will understand what her child is experiencing.

To bring it to a close we do a short exercise around this.

⚓ Reflection

Looking back I could have stopped after Ana first saw her son as a young adult. Yet I go on and ask whether she has more children. Then meaningful things happen again. Sometimes I do not know why I do what I do, but it appears to be worthwhile. This is an example of that phenomenon.

Parents should not to go with their worries to their children. That burdens those children with something that is not theirs and therefore they cannot do anything with. Systemically this places the children in the position of the parents and the parents in that of the children. With nobody in their own place the system is seriously weakened. Parents have a child's place with their own parents. There they can raise their fears and worries. Parents understand what their child is going through. That supports the child.

Observing that she displayed the same concerns as her mother towards her own child would have been a nice systemic opening: What happened in the family that being worried and afraid occupy such a prominent place?

1.2 Belonging and order

Being living systems, organisations need to be complete and in order. There is a place available for each part that belongs to the whole of the system. And each part should occupy its own place. Not more, not less, not different. That gives peace and strength to the whole. Exclusion of parts, disorder, or a partly disturbed order leads to loss of energy in the organisation. That is what we explore in the following three cases.

⚊O Just buy some different chairs

Fernanda and Luis, both aged 25, have long been a couple and, two years ago, they started a business together: designing and producing contemporary clothes for young people. "We started the company after we won a design prize." They now employ five people and want to take the next growth step.

Luis is creative director and Fernanda is the CEO and handles all the management issues. They want to talk to me because the company is in such a mess and communication is really poor. Almost nobody listens to Fernanda, and Luis listens to her only occasionally.

"Did you win the prize together," is my initial question. No, of course Luis won it; the creative mind.

"Who is or are the owners?" Luis owns 51% and Fernanda 21% of the shares. So there are some other smaller shareholders. "Would you say, then, that Luis started the company and is the number one?" They both confirm this.

"If creativity is the core of what keeps the company afloat, I think it's conceivable that there is little or no interest in rules, agreements, invoicing, recording what you do and things like that. After all, they only inhibit creativity and, anyway, they're unimportant." Luis glows when I say this.

Fernanda jumps up when I say: "If the company wants to ensure its survival, many things need to be agreed and in place. That seems exactly the dilemma you are facing. Both your qualities are needed. And you Luis, as the No.1, must create the right conditions.

Fernanda says that people who are unhappy with her decisions go behind her back and sort it out with Luis. There is even someone who refuses to talk to Fernanda; up till now they have allowed this behaviour.

To Fernanda I say: "Would you put up with Luis' behaviour if you didn't love him?" "No, of course not, but I love him so much." Earlier my eyes were drawn to Fernanda's shoes: sneakers with shiny steel points on the toes. "Who is it you want to kick?" Her eyes, shining with love, focus on Luis.

Then I give a short lesson about systemic work:
"Luis, as the founder and number one you must make it clear to everyone that Fernanda is the CEO and that people must listen to her. And this applies to you also! Better that you call her 'the CEO' than Fernanda. You have to give the right example. Send people to her when their issues are business related; then have nothing more to do with them. Never reverse any of her decisions, certainly not in little tête-à-têtes with others. Every time you do that, you're basically saying that there is no place in the business for Fernanda.

And if that is so, then you have to tell her directly in a dialogue with her and take responsibility for the consequences.

Fernanda, if you do not get from Luis the place you need to make your appropriate contribution, you have to leave. And when Luis acts with good intentions, and sometimes makes a mess, you have to take appropriate action. Since he has appointed you as CEO, you have that authority and you have to use it."

To both: "It really is difficult for you to combine your love for each other with your very different qualities, and the company desperately needs both."

We also discussed what would be a good time to get the staff together and clarify precisely who is responsible for what. That became clear quickly. Fernanda began laughing loudly when she imagined meeting with everyone and said: "We only have chairs with wheels and everyone always shoots around in all directions."

My response: "That fits perfectly with creativity. But if you have some money left you might consider buying different chairs for your business meetings."

⊤—O Reflection

Besides factual statements about what their business produces they tell me very quickly that it is a mess. To me that immediately suggests order. Does everyone and everything in this system take the place that's there for him or her and which is recognized as the place from which they can make the best possible contribution to the whole?

So, when it is said that 'we' have won a prize, this raises in me the question of whether it is said that way from a shared pride in the company, or that it shows here what is so evident in the bigger picture, the mess. Therefore, I ask if they have won the prize together. In their response we find the first issue of ordering.

I rather prefer to speak about functions and places than about the individuals who occupy these places. Systems have places; people occupy them temporarily.

Clothing, jewellery, attitude, behaviour, for me are all elements that I register with this question at the back of my mind: of what greater whole are these, perhaps, a reflection? The whole makes itself continuously visible in the parts. In that respect, from the beginning, Fernanda's shoes grabbed the most of my attention. Hence my question about them.

Circumstances, behaviour, words, they all do something with me and I let myself be guided by this in what I say or ask. It's not like I set out to investigate. It happens to me.
What I always do is ask myself: does this say something

more about me or more about the coachee? If it's the first, then I let it rest.

At their request, the conversation was about the company. Therefore, I limited myself to that. I did not notice any invitation to talk about their relationship. It seems to me inevitable that something similar is at play in their personal contact with each other and who takes which place there. But if they have no questions, I do not discuss it.

As I write this, I wonder how long and at what price relationships and family businesses exist? What has each to do to create sufficient systemic balance? Who pays which price?

⊶ Who's number 1 here?

During a workshop a woman asks if I want to work with her. She sits down next to me and starts talking about the family business where they just can't succeed in appointing a suitable CEO. If I take my eyes off her and look around, at the back of the room I see a woman gesturing. My questioning gaze goes to and fro between the woman in the room and the one next to me. "That's my sister," she says. Who also seems to work in the family business. "Come over and sit down here, please," I say to her. She does and I ask: "What we've just seen here between you, does that also happen in the business?" Well, it turns out that is the case and results in the remaining two sisters (also waving) coming forward from the back of the room.

It raises these questions in my mind: What is asking for attention here, what else belongs here, and is everything in its right place?

"Who is the oldest in the family? And who has which place in the company?" They interrupt each other regularly while attempting to explain how it is. What is finally unravelled, after much intervention from me, is this. Father started the business and one brother, now deceased, worked in it. Not all the sisters started in the business at the same time. It turns out to concern not one but two companies, the second of which is an offspring from the first. In each company, everybody has a different position, and not everyone works in both businesses. (No wonder they behave the way they do! What a wonderful reflection of everyday reality.)

I remark: "How nice that you haven't found a CEO yet. He or she would need a more stable situation than you currently offer, despite your good intentions."

They would like to get on with my proposal, to make a start with putting things in order. I ask them to sit from left to right, clockwise, in order of age. In the appropriate places, empty chairs are placed for the father (the founder of the company) and for the deceased brother. They all take turns saying: "My name is . . . In the family, I'm number. . . " And to each of the others: "In the family you are number . . ." I start with the oldest, of course, and then continue in order of age.

I let them speak out the same ordering for the first business, and then for the second: "In the first company, I'm number one; in the family, I'm number. . . In the second company, I'm number. . . " and so forth.

For now this really is enough. It was hard work just to get started with the order. Too bad that two days later I'm sitting in the plane home. I really ought to have granted them more time.

⊶ Reflection

Did I let myself get too carried away, in all the hustle and bustle; an outsider firmly taking control of creating some order? Albeit from the well-intentioned idea that they needed it. But the coach who means well - by knowing what the client's system needs - does not strengthen the system.

The last sentences in the story of this case elicit this remark from a colleague who reads the draft: Daddy! How come I did not realize I was working so hard to find a solution? Where and through what did I lose my professional detachment? Now I ask myself questions like: maybe I represented the father, or brother? Did I want to save four women at once? Was I, unconsciously, happy once again to be asked for one of my other qualities: creating order out of chaos?

In retrospect, I regret that I did not ask what was produced in the two companies. All I can do is just be open to the possibility that this might also play a role in what happened.

⌐━O Leaving the system

Sometimes it is voluntary, sometimes it is forced; someone leaves his place in an organisation. The key is to leave nothing behind that you ought to take with you and let go of what no longer belongs to you. On the organisation's side something similar is needed; does one do enough to really let the person in question go and to make the place free for a successor?

In general, what I find exciting and enjoyable about coaching is stepping into the completely unknown territory which a coachee brings and then, relying on my awareness and with my systemic knowledge in the back of my mind, asking questions and occasionally making comments through which the coachee comes to realise what's going on. Sometimes, however, it is simply a matter of telling someone what he could do if he wants to pay attention to system dynamics. Here is an example of such a situation.

⌐━O A death

A consultant is supporting a team. One of the team members is terminally ill, and comes to work only now and then; his life will end soon. The consultant wants to know how she can support the team around the imminent death of the team member: "What needs to happen in the team is, systemically to say goodbye to him. In a practical sense, what can I do to help?"

My response: Get everyone together in a full team meeting and ask everyone to sit, clockwise starting from the team leader, in order of their number of years in the team. The one working in this team the longest is first, clockwise, to the left of the team leader, and so on ending with the one who joined the team most recently. It is the role of the team leader to thank the person who will 'leave' for all he has contributed to the goal and work of the team. It is also worthwhile to recognize what it cost him. A third element is that the team leader makes it clear they will continue with the work in their own way, always remembering that this person, who soon will disappear from the team, made a contribution to how it is now; even if it they go in a completely different direction. Team members do something similar and so does the person.

At the first meeting after the death of the team member, the team should sit in the same order, but leaving an empty seat in the place where the deceased previously sat. This is a good time, quietly and respectfully, to reflect on the death and share with everyone what it means for each person. It also helps to state that there is a new, empty place. At the beginning of the next meeting the team leader could move the empty seat and place it to the left of the person who has been in the team for the shortest time: the place for a new team member.

1.3 Propelling force

If the basic needs of a living system - which an organisation is - are not met, then the system automatically generates 'warning' signals, symptoms of what is missing. Which we easily see and experience as problems. But, at the systemic level, these problems are solutions for something. But for what? And how do you find out?

Helping questions are:
- o For what might this problem be a good solution?
- o Suppose that the 'problem' was solved, what would be badly missed?
- o If the issue no longer existed, what parts of the system would immediately bring it back to life?

Many organisations have a vision and a mission, through which the organisation expresses what they want to be or where they want to go. Their aim is to guide the whole. And often it will be pretty difficult for an organisation to realise the vision and mission they have formulated.

But there is also the propelling force, also known as the guiding principle, and it exists in the organisation as a much stronger force, and it is followed because people are unconsciously loyal to it. Usually there is talk of some propelling forces in an organisation. The leader should then clarify the hierarchy of these forces.

The propelling force derives from what the organisation is at its core. This theme is at play in the following conversations.

⟜⊕ We only stay for a short time

The manager of a home for the disabled complains about high turnover among employees. "Everyone who comes to work here is gone again within a year. It's my job to change this. We need new employees to stay longer." It turns out that only two, out of a staff of twenty, have been here more than a couple of years.

When I ask when this situation began, she replies that it's always been like this. And then I ask what typifies the residents. It is a home where children usually stay less than a year and then are relocated somewhere into the following age group.

That elicits an observation: "For the children – for whom the house is intended – the following seems to apply: we only stay here for a short time." Surprised by the way I put it, the manager admits it is true.

I continue: "Could you say that it represents the core of the home – You are only here for a short time. And if that is the case, perhaps it might be impossible to stay longer, for employees too. In other words: employees who leave quickly honour the guiding principle, the propelling force of the organization. What a beautiful demonstration of loyalty to the main principle of the home!"

The manager is open to this line of thinking but, somewhat impatiently, asks the question: "Yes, and what must I do now to make employees stay longer?"

I give her two options to consider: abandon this wish, and so allow yourselves to continue acting in accordance with the propelling force; or else investigate the history of the home and how it was founded. And in the latter case, look to understand what the deepest intentions of the founder were and how they might be the source of 'You'll only stay here for a short time.' "And if you discover something there, it is good to recognize that it just was that way, that it has made a good contribution, and that now the time has come when it is good for the children that staff stay longer." It serves the whole, when everyone leaves with the children that which belongs with the children, and takes their own place with everything that belongs to that place.

Through acknowledgement of what was, in addition to recognition of what is, new energy is allowed to flow.

⌐—⊕ Reflection

The question of when the problem started and what was going on at that time, are questions about facts and circumstances. I don't ask why the problem arose. That would be detective work: looking for explanations and guilt perhaps. I pose my kind of questions to determine whether the presenting problem might really be in response to a systemic need of the organisation.

If there is no clear period or event that seems to have been the origin of the problem, then maybe it has something to do with the founder or the setting-up of the organisation. What was transmitted in the genes of the system?

☛ "With us there is always a place for everyone."

Kees is head of HR, and says that the organisation has an interim Admin Manager whose contract expires soon and that there is uncertainty about whether it will be renewed. "He's not really doing the job well and it seems to be too much for him. And yet he is a competent person."

Has anything unusual ever happened around the role of the Admin Manager was my first thought, and that leads to the question: "What happened to his predecessor?" Kees says that the first Admin Manager retired with his pension after just three years.

My response: "This function hasn't been in place for very long. Why is that?" "The previous director no longer wanted to have individual consultations with all the staff members, so he put a person in between." I continue with: "And appointed someone whom it was clear would not stay very long." Seeing another possible pattern I ask: "Does this happen more often?"

"I do not know. What I do know is that company gossip says everyone thinks that the director arranged this very nicely for that particular employee."

"You mean the function was created, perhaps, in order to provide a place for someone to see out his years and ensure his pension?" "Yes, actually everyone in the organisation sees it that way."

Still looking for what might be happening in the organisation, I ask: "Does it often happen that functions are created for people? And if so, what problem is solved by doing that? Or perhaps pushed out of sight?"

Kees says at least it avoids having to lay people off. For me this begs the question: "Are you an organisation that runs with the hare and the hounds, that tries to stay on good terms with everybody?" His response: "We are an organisation that helps people who are in trouble and have nowhere else to go."

I make that a bit stronger: "If I put it concisely, it seems that it is the nature of this organisation to prioritize individual needs above the organisation's interests. If this is true then it really would be strange if a function was not created for someone who has only a couple of years left."

After some silence, Kees says he now realizes that in their organisation work is fitted to the people, rather than the other way round. I want to return to the staff. It turns out that this not-so-very-large organisation has a rather large admin department. Unusual, I think: "What kind of people are in that department?" "A single specialist and the rest are mostly former managers." "Managers without portfolio? Running with the hare and hounds again? Always a place for everyone - again?" Kees looks startled and says: "Oh, it sounds pretty heavy when you say it like that."

I go back to the beginning, realising that something seems to be clinging onto the place of the Admin Manager and say: "The director did not want to meet individual staff members, and so he created the Admin Manager function." When I ask if I may enlarge on this, Kees nods. "Okay, I'll make it really big. The director creates a role that separates him from the staff. Could the message have been, 'I do not want the staff!' And if that were so, then there is no one who can properly fulfil the Admin Manager's role, because there is simply no place for him or her. The organisation appears to have been subservient to the first manager. And once the original task was completed, there was no longer a need for the function."

There's a long silence and then: "Oh. Initially I hoped you might have some useful ideas for arranging the succession, but this is going much further. I need some time to think about this."

Six months later, at a railway station, I bump into Kees, who says that the interim manager is still working there. My response: "And for what is that a very good solution?" "Ah," he says, "it's become so clear to me that we are an organisation that is very good at caring for. We even do this for consultants with whom we are dissatisfied. With us, everybody gets another chance. Just like our clients. Long ago, that was the motivation of the organisation's founders."

⌐○ Reflection

What has happened earlier to the place? That is a logical first question for me, instead of going into the qualities of the person who holds the position. If it turns out that the function only recently came into being, and there was only one person holding that place, that brings me quickly to the question about the origin of the function. It seems to me that there clearly is a chair on which the interim manager sits, but systemically the place might not even exist. And then gradually it becomes visible how this manifests in this system. To the beautiful last sentences of the coachee on the platform.

It is incredible how much trouble can be caused just by loyalty to the founding principles of the organisation. People are ready to pay a high price.

1.4 Systems confusion

Behaviour that is appropriate in one system, can create disorder in another system. For example, a manager can deal with employees as if they are (his) children. An employee can approach his manager as if he's his father.

In coaching it helps to be alert to the attitude and words of the coachee: e.g. are they exhibiting the professional relationship between manager and employee or coach and client? How I feel as the coach is a great source of information: Do I feel like I'm becoming a child, dependent, or am I just getting paternal or maternal feelings via what the coachee is saying?

Commercial relationships can also manifest much that is a parent - child relationship. An example is the salesman who praises his products so highly because he believes they really are good for his clients. If he earns a good income from it because many people get a lot of pleasure from his way of selling, why not? When as a salesman you are not successful, you might investigate in what place your behaviour puts your customer. It can, therefore, be quite helpful to keep different systems apart. The following conversations are about this issue.

↤⊗ I miss my children

Carola is 48 years old. Along with her husband she has a training and consultancy company in a big city. They often work with NLP, constellations, coaching with horses and activities in nature. Every Saturday afternoon and evening they work for free with fifteen children from an orphanage. Every six months they start a new group.

Carola has developed a follow-up training course for the hundreds of participants from previous courses. She offers deepening of the work in several areas. There are modules that she or her husband delivers, and for others they bring in renowned trainers and teachers. The course has ten modules. The first three modules had only 5, 6 and 1 participant respectively. Carola has no idea why there is so little enthusiasm.

My first question: "With what key objective did you create this deepening program?" She talks enthusiastically about how she loves to give her participants the chance to learn even more: "They're such wonderful and valuable modules! People will get so much from them!"

I feel a bit like a little child whose mother is saying: "Just do what I tell you, it's good for you." Inevitably this leads to my next comment: "From your professional knowledge you have ideas about what might be of use to these people. The flavour of your message carries a bit of I know what's good for you, and that reminds me of a mother patronizing her child. It seems to be more about your needs than those of potential participants."

Touched, her first reaction is: "Yes, that's how I offer it to them; I love caring for them." After a long time of silence, for both of us, she continues: "I married very young and very soon had two children. When they left home - quite a few years ago now - my world collapsed. I could not imagine my life without being able to care for the children." Then she starts crying and adds: "Actually, that's still the case. I miss them so much." I mention that perhaps she has found a good solution in their Saturday orphans group, but that adult customers need something else. And we talk for a while about that. The result of the conversation is that Carola is going to do some market research among her customers.

⊗⟶ Reflection

Often I am happy with the effects of my silence. I have learned to be silent. Because, sometimes, I do not know how to proceed. Coachees always start talking again and, not infrequently, they lay their cards very clearly on the table, enabling me to continue.

⚿ "Daddy, where are you?"

Amanda works at a multinational company and has had management positions in various countries. She says that they have been lonely posts and she found that difficult. She is now working in her own country but she still feels lonely. She wonders what she should do to get the regional director more interested in her work: "I feel so alone."

Lonely jobs, feeling alone; I wonder when that started and so I ask her a question. "When in the past have you felt alone, abandoned? When you were little?" She does her best to protect her makeup from a few tears. "You won't save it," I say, "your mascara's running everywhere." A tear, a smile and a pair of black stripes are the result.

After a bit of tidying up we get serious again. "Daddy, where are you? Is or was that an important question for you?" She appears to have missed him very much.

"Well, it seems like you are experiencing the same thing in your work! And you know, that you miss your father can never be fixed. This pain exists and is a part of you and your life. That hole will never be filled. What perhaps is not necessary is that you keep on seeking that same pain. You've had enough solitude. And you give no pleasure to your father by, in this distracted way, still continuing to look for him. He was not there in the way that you needed, and you just have to get on with it. Perhaps now is the time to say: Daddy, out of love for you and myself I am stopping searching for you. It was the way it was."

I get the impression that she's taken the message in, but that it confuses her. I think that's logical. I propose that we stop for now and if she wants to come back to this later, she is welcome.

🔑 Reflection

Adults who struggle with existential themes, such as in this case, often find the origin back in their early childhood. For an unmet need from that time, a solution will still be sought. Looking for the source I therefore pose the question: "When also have you felt alone?"
We could have looked at another systemic dimension with the question: What happened in your family around travelling, leaving places, being lonely? Who has, perhaps, felt really uprooted?

When have I done enough as a coach? Did I need to do more, to go further? I realize that, personally, I run the risk of stopping too early rather than going on too long. That's me. My idea is that if one step is taken, a new seed planted, time is needed for what might ensue. All in good time and confident that the person is going to do what is right for him or her.

⚷ Your baby is a mature professional

Enrique, along with his wife, is a successful entrepreneur. He has a problem he cannot solve. A year ago they created a Communications & PR function. And since that moment it has not worked. They have already appointed a second person to the role but that also hasn't worked out. Both he and his wife are very dissatisfied.

"Who did this work before it became a separate function?" is my first question. There's pride and joy in his voice when he says: "My wife and I did it together." I say, "It sounds like you two found it a very nice job." He agrees.

"Could you say that this function is your baby, and you are really fond of it?" I've hit the bullseye. I ask him, spontaneously, without thinking, to answer the question I'm about to ask: "How old is your baby now?" He immediately replies: "Five years old." Instantly I get an urge to sit on the ground.

I invite him to sit on the ground with me like a pair of five-year-olds. We both feel an impulse to play.

Enrique is shocked and understands immediately where the problem lies. They are approaching the new staff member as a small child.
We go back to sitting on our chairs. I ask him how he could change the five-year-old's playroom into a workplace for an independent professional. Very soon he has a picture: it's a revolving chair that you turn the seat to adjust the height; and he makes that movement. He adds: "The height difference is considerable."

I invite him to place two chairs in such a way that we – I represent the employee and he is himself as the owner of the company – can do our jobs well. Some puzzling and pushing chairs around follows. The best situation for the employee is when Enrique says: "This is your job. I hired you because of your expertise. Get on with it." And then he walks away from me and sits entirely somewhere else. What a relief we both feel!

Finally I suggest he tells his wife about this and they bring about the changes together: "If one owner keeps seeing the function as a small child and the other sees the function as mature and independent, systemically it will not get any easier for the function."

⚷ Reflection

I learned to follow the impulses that I feel to do or say things. Embarrassment has thus been superseded by daring to do it and to letting go again if it does not work. It's my awareness and I let whatever happens percolate through me. I allow it. And I am as surprised as the coachee about how and what manifests.

1.5 Other themes

⊷ Carrying your own load is enough

"Carry your own load" is a good systemic motto. If each bears his own load, that also helps keep the relationship strong, as is clear in the case of Carlos, who is struggling with a dilemma that he just cannot solve. He is in his early twenties and, sitting in the midst of his fellow students, he asks a question: "I would really like to take a step in my life; but if I do so I will disappoint my parents terribly. And I don't want to hurt them that way. What's the right thing for me to do?"

I ask Carlos if he is being honest with himself in the step he would like to take. Very firmly, he confirms he is.

"Then it's time to gather all your courage and take the step," I tell him. "If you lead your life honestly and sincerely, that's the only thing you can do. That it hurts your parents is not your responsibility. That is their issue. You show your love for them by not wanting to hurt them. That's what you can keep telling them and letting them feel: I love you and I will live my own life. Be prepared that, for a while at least, and perhaps a very long time, they might not accept your decision. And there's also the chance that their reaction to you might turn out to be better than expected."

Carlos nods vigorously and waves his hands to indicate that this is enough.

⊙—╪ Reflection

I do not need more than for the coachee to tell that he wants to take a step and that there is something that stops him doing so. If I start asking exactly what it is all about, I risk being pulled away from my systemic orientation. A step further with Carlos would have been to examine what systemic loyalty prevents him from growing to maturity and living his own life.

▆━▌ Who does it?

Her childhood had not been easy; her relationship with her mother remains complicated.

"Sometimes my mom drives me crazy, really crazy," said a young woman during the coaching conversation.

My response: "That's not true. Your being driven crazy is the best possible response from you, at that moment, to what your mother does."

▐━▀ Reflection

I do understand that it feels like her mother is doing it to her. My observation that her response is the best she could do, points the way to how she can take responsibility for what she does. And of course she also asks why on earth her mother does what she does. Well, as a daughter that is a totally inappropriate statement! That belongs absolutely with the mother, who obviously acts from her own background, loyalties and patterns.

For me this is an example of a systemic intervention: something that allows every part of a whole - here the mother/daughter system – to resume its right place. Taking your own place and being responsible for yourself creates strong people and vital organisations. I left it here because the message was loud and clear and, in my estimation, opened up new possibilities for the coachee. The next step could be to ask: What is the systemic contribution her craziness makes to the family system.

☐─● Four minutes

John is a big, friendly man. After he sits, and we have looked quietly at each other, in answer to my question about what brings him here he replies: "My wife sent me."

"Okay, and what's your question for me?"

"I wouldn't know," is his response. He adds a couple of sentences to say that he enjoys his work and his family.

Triggered by the possible existence of a pattern I decide to pose only one question; if it doesn't have any meaning for him then we're done. I ask him if he often does things at the instigation of his wife or someone else, things he wouldn't do without pressure from someone else.

This happens often to him with his wife and he has no problem with that: "That's how it is. It's a matter of giving and taking in the relationship. I think it's a good way to live together."

I say that we have finished our conversation, and that's totally fine with me. He feels uncomfortable and apologizes repeatedly for the fact that the appointment was made. I repeat my comment and then get up from my chair. I offer my hand as a goodbye, and I say: "You know, if I was in your shoes I too would feel uneasy. And for me, the best thing we can do now is stop."

⚏—→ Reflection

Where there's no question, there's no work for me.

2 Background

The following section comes from of the book

Systemic Consulting
The organisation as a living system

By Siebke Kaat and Anton de Kroon

Publisher: Uitgeverij Het Noorderlicht

www.hetnoorderlicht.com

available at Amazon

ISBN 1522956832

2.1 Characteristics of systemic coaching

Systemic coaching has several characteristics:

o The systemic coach, just like the systemic consultant, uses his awareness as information. Completely open and without judgement, he exposes himself to what arises in him through his contact with the client and the bigger whole to which the client belongs.

o He always works from his systemic attitude, conscious of the fact that he contributes best by seeing everyone and everything in the context of the whole. He does not join in the client's judgements about colleagues, the management or the organisation. He does not want to solve anything. Together with his client he wants to look at what appears from the system, what happens to the client in that organisational system and what, potentially, the client could do to take his place in a better way. He resists the temptation to portray himself as the expert, the helper or the saviour of the client or the system as a whole.

o Always, he puts any question about an individual in the context of the whole of the system. It is for this whole that he works.

o With his systemic radar, he permanently scans all the parts and the system as a whole. He is on the alert for anything to do with the belonging or excluding of parts, the order, the place his client is taking (or has been given) and the history of that place.

- He is attentive to what is repeating itself, both in the person and work of the client, and in the organisation within and for which he is working.

- His efforts are aimed at enabling the client to discover the dynamics of which he is a part.

- He regards problems as symptoms that just want to show, systemically, where the shoe pinches. So the content of a client's story rarely contains the real issue: it is only the wrapping ... around the gift of a systemic phenomenon. The coach should regularly ask himself this question. For what is this problem a good solution?

Contracting

Systemic coaching is oriented at getting the client to look from a systemic perspective at his question, his place and his situation. By doing so, he might recognise his personal patterns in 'his' organisational systems. Or he might be able to see that some of his behaviour expresses his loyalty to someone or something from his family of origin. By looking without judgement, transcending patterns can become clear. Sometimes one session is enough, sometimes more are needed. But it is the client who decides this, not the coach. The coach's place is beside the client. He does not guide the client, he only facilitates a process in which the client can look at his situation in a different way and can then act differently. By deciding for himself, how often and with what frequency sessions will take place, the client takes the lead. The systemic coach lets go of that.

Finding the root of the problem

In systemic coaching the first question is, always, in which system will we find the root of the problem. Does what is being experienced as a problem relate more to the person or more to the organisation? Or is it, by chance, related to both systems?

When it appears to belong more to the person, systems confusion might be the issue: someone in the organisation is behaving as he used to behave at home, when he was younger. Irrespective of his work environment, he takes his place – in relation to his colleagues and management – in the same way he did in the past with his siblings and/or parents. Often, the client recognises the problems it causes and has experienced similar problems in previous work situations. Whenever someone else, temporarily or permanently, took his place, that newcomer did not experience these problems; predecessors did not encounter them either. These are signals that the issue originates more from the family context than the organisational. An indication that the problem is likely to be more related to the organisation is when the client tells you that what is happening to him is really strange. He hardly knows it or does not know it at all. Further inquiry can reveal that others, in similar roles, run into similar issues. Then it is very likely that it belongs to the organisation. A different person, in the same role, would almost certainly experience the same problem.

And then of course there is the mix of both. The organisational and the personal. With their own typical patterns both, somehow, attract each other. The pattern of one fulfils a need of the other and vice versa.
You might ask yourself this question: To what extent is the choosing of a job, or the choosing of an employee, an act of free

will? Sometimes it looks as if each is being pulled towards the other like magnets. Magnets that believe they are acting autonomously!

2.2 Systemic-phenomenological basis

The knowledge from which I operate as a systemic coach includes insights into family and organisational systems, which I have gained, since the beginning of this century, through study, education, training and experience.

In both systems – mostly unconsciously – it involves issues such as:
- o loyalty (or lack of loyalty) to the system's origins,
- o recognition or denial of its history,
- o belonging to or exclusion from the system,
- o taking or not taking the place each system has for each part,
- o balance between taking and giving.

Both systems share characteristics such as:
- o orientation to survive and to reach their destiny,
- o being part of a greater whole,
- o orientation towards both conservation and exchange,
- o self-regulation by which the system creates signals and solutions.

Whatever they need to function fully, family and organisational systems show through signs and symptoms. This is often difficult to understand, because they are easily perceived as unwelcome problems which people want to avoid. Systemically that would make the problems even worse.

2.3 My task

As a systemic coach I regard it as my task to, in a way, take the client on a tour of his own house; where he has lived for so long. I point to doors that he might not yet have opened, or rooms that he doesn't know exist. Often it comes down to pointing to doors that link two existing rooms.

It is the client who decides whether he opens the door and enters the rooms. Sometimes he opens the door but cannot find the light switch. If he asks where it is, I tell him. Whether he actually turns the light on is completely up to him.

With this pointing at doors, saying what kind of space is behind them, explaining how any furniture in the room might be used - if required - the coaching comes to an end. It usually takes twenty to thirty minutes, sometimes less, rarely more.

I also see myself as a three-dimensional movie screen in which all the aforementioned systemic issues and characteristics are included, like mountains with rock and ice formations, icy north walls and charming southern slopes, valleys with streams, rivers, paths and roads, villages, towns and so forth. Upon that screen the coachee projects the film of his story.

Personally, I am not only that film screen but - from a distance - I also look at it and I experience the film - without me being in it. Then work can be done, in this cinema of life.

2.4 Awareness

Even before the coaching starts, I focus on my awareness. What's happening in and with me in the very first contact with the coachee? That came perhaps via email, a phone call or a meeting in a different context. I register what it brings up in me. I do not lock myself into an opinion or judgment. In all candour I ask myself: the way things happen here, and what that does to me, if that would happen more often for what might it be an example? From what (unconscious) systemic need of the coachee's system does it stem, and what does it give him or her? There is a very good reason for the coachee to do what he does, to have the problem that he has. As yet I don't know the background to the coachee's behaviour and usually he doesn't either. But I'm curious about it. There's a big chance that it will help him further if he gets clarity around that, and can give everything the place it deserves.

I'm always watching my own observations and feelings. It's as if I'm neither looking at the other, nor at what happens, but that seeing is happening. And then things fall in place. How the coachee enters; what he looks like; his first words and sentences; how he walks; how he sits; does he move his chair around or not; how does he look around and breathe; his complexion; what he does with his legs, arms, hands and feet. Does he look directly at me? I often think of Bert Hellinger's observation: in the client's first words is the resolution to his question.

What it is about for me is discovering whether, with the help of my perception and observation, something seems to fall into place for the coachee.

2.5 Attitude

There are some attitudinal approaches that characterise how I work as a systemic coach, and which I'll explain briefly.

Working without judgements

Usually, the coachee has had to deal with enough opinions and judgments – i.e. convictions – before he starts a coaching engagement. Perhaps mostly from himself. Repeating the same judgements, or making new ones, does not help bring the coachee back into his own strength. It is not the coach but the coachee who is the expert on his system. Only then, and at his request, can the aforementioned tour of his house take place. And, in every part of the house, I can be open and wait in stillness while I consider the question of what moved the builder to build it this way, and what moved the resident to live in it this way. So, in the coachee I see both the builder and the resident.

If I notice that I'm the one judging I don't fight that, because it would be systemically counterproductive. A system opposes any attempt to exclude any of its parts.
The first thing I have to do is recognize and acknowledge that I have judgements and that means I'm biased. It is the movement of acknowledging that there is what there is. It's then my choice whether or not I act upon it. Sometimes, before starting to work, I make conscious contact with my judgments. I thank them for the fact that they are there, tell them I am grateful for the good things they have brought me so far and ask them to stay with me, even if I do not actively involve them in the encounter that I am about to have with a coachee.
For me judgements are also related to the fact that I already think I know what the problem is and how to solve it.

Concerned and withdrawn

No matter how terrible the problem of a coachee might be, I look further, into the systemic factors that might be the cause.

Being present and involved in the suffering of the coachee is tremendously valuable when it is combined with detachment and restraint. It brings me close to the coachee without losing myself in him, realising that if I were him, I really would do exactly the same. And that's a whole different meaning to what everyone understands when someone says, 'If I were you, I'd ...', followed by a recommendation of what the other would do if he were you. But he's not you ...

Multilaterally partial

By being 'partial' to all sides, I commit myself as a coach to every part of the whole that is involved. I'm not neutral or impartial. I put myself in the place of each of the elements involved, including the forgotten or excluded parts, and I look from there to the whole, of which, till now, a coachee might only have seen a part.

2.6 What I often do

There are a few movements that I often use during coaching. These are steps in the process of change that I experience as helpful. Partly for myself, because they keep me focused, and partly for the coachee because they help him to find and take his own path.

Stop

Coachees are usually very willing to tell carefully and exactly what they are suffering from and why they came. Even though this might be accompanied by statements like: "I find it hard to tell exactly what is going on."

It often happens that I interrupt the coachee's story. My interest as a systemic coach goes to the greater whole. Not the details and emotions that many coachees tend to describe because they are so used to doing so. I unlearned to keep listening politely when my feelings tell me that I would be better off stopping. As soon as I notice this happening with details or emotions from the coachee's story, I say, for example: "Thank you for what you said. What I need is to know if you have experienced something similar more often. Is that perhaps the case?"

Of what greater whole is this a reflection?

Of course coachees talk about incidents and emotions. I do not get involved in this. They have been extremely busy themselves, at that level, and obviously have not found a solution. My contribution is the perspective from a systemic level. This might be a bit harsh, but it's never really about what the coachee is telling. It's about looking further, deeper.

What is this an example of? When did it start, and what were the circumstances? What happened, what are the facts? Has it happened before? These are the kind of questions that pop up in many cases.

Embrace what you want to avoid

Whoever asks for coaching has, one way or another, a serious problem, often formulated in terms of 'wanting to get rid of it'. The coachee is, therefore, my only point of engagement. I'm not going to change his boss or his mother or him for that matter. If he wants me to, I can help him understand what might be going on and how he could do things differently.

It starts with facing the fact that the present problem was once a wonderful solution for something, and has been of great service to the coachee and / or the system to which he belongs. For example, as a child you ensured the life-preserving love of your parents by doing everything they wanted and never having your own will. If you still do that at your work - because you literally do not know better - you'll be the laughingstock of the department. And, of course, you'll do anything to get away from that.

But there was a time when that behaviour contributed to your survival. Therefore it has earned recognition and thanks. It is about a part of yourself. Therefore, it strengthens the system if that part is also recognized and appreciated for what it has contributed. More so if it no longer needs to be active for the coachee. It has played its part.

Walking a new path

The movement of recognition and appreciation might not actually make it possible for you to let go of the old behaviour, but for the old behaviour to let you go. That it is able to let go of you because it got from you what it needed systemically: to be seen as a part of the whole to which it belongs. And where the original behaviour ran in parallel with unconscious love for your parents, those two can now exist separately. You can keep loving your parents, let them see your love and, at the same time, try behaving differently.

In these situations I always use the word and. If but were used, it would – for me - totally undermine the whole of the previous movement.

Silences

Silences are a beautiful gift. Then I sit back in my chair and think to myself: yes, he is at work! At some point the other person always resumes talking or, in some other way, communicating with me. If it takes a very long time I do, to make contact again, sometimes ask: "What's happening for you?"

What does it say about me if I sometimes cannot stand the silence? Is it that I can no longer restrain myself from helping?

Expanding

I often expand on or sharpen what the other says, in order to clarify the core of the issue. Usually, I introduce it with great emphasis: "If it would be that ..., then ... And maybe it is completely different. I'm not saying it is exactly as I say, but maybe something touches the core." Whenever I have said something this way, I'm usually quiet until the coachee says something. Or I ask a question like: "Does it ring a bell somewhere? Or not?" If the latter is the case, I urge him to forget the whole story. Several times I have seen someone come back later and say, "When I thought about it a bit more..."

I take one step and then I move along

I try to go from just a single event into the systemic dimension. A coachee says, for example, that he feels not seen in his work: "No one in the team takes me into account." Then my next step could be to ask: "Where else have you felt not seen?" This question stems from consciously weighing my systemic knowledge, in search of the greater whole of which the story is just one example.

Then I stop and connect, from inside, with some larger, older, more comprehensive whole, whatever it might have been.
Then the idea can incubate at bit until a question comes like: "At home, were there many children and were you perhaps the last?" And, not in advance, but more as I'm pronouncing the words, I realise that such a situation could easily lead to not being seen.

If I get a negative answer I let go of the idea and wait for the next inspiration.

Farewell

For now, we're done. It's time to leave my office. Work awaits.

I hope your visit has inspired you to find your own way of coaching and working.

Good luck.

Anton de Kroon
ak@hellingerinstituut.nl

About the author: Anton de Kroon

In the early eighties, I trained as a coach and since then, in companies and with individual clients, I have coached countless people. Early this century, I read my first books by Bert Hellinger; it opened a new world for me into which I soon went deeper and deeper. First I trained in family constellations. I was, at that time, working as a management consultant (co-owner of Greep Management and Organisational Development) and excited about transferring the underlying ideas behind family constellations to organisations. Learning to facilitate organisational constellations was an unavoidable next step. As was the permanent further training in systemic-phenomenological work. As a management consultant and coach, I developed ways to use the ideas behind constellations in an advisory or coaching session without necessarily doing a constellation.

This led to co-authoring, with Siebke Kaat, Systemic Consulting: The organisation as a living system, and providing training and workshops in systemic interventions for the Dutch Bert Hellinger Institute, in the Netherlands and abroad. The next logical step was to employ my growing systemic insight more and more in my coaching. One of the results is this book.

'Problems are solutions' is a popular starting point for me. During a coaching session, clients often respond with: "I've never looked at it that way ..."
Looking differently, through the systemic lens, is what continues to fascinate me.

About the (systemic) editor:
James Campbell

Most editors set out to 'correct' a text, mistakenly believing that the author doesn't know what they are saying. I see myself in service of the story, then the author, using all my intuition, learning and feeling (and, if needed, grammar, punctuation, syntax etc.) to ensure their intentions arrive with the reader clear and intact. I'm constantly checking (with myself and the author) that my opinions, beliefs and ideas are not slipping into the book unnoticed, at the same time trying to give the story flow, removing ambiguity and adding clarity.

In this work there comes a point in the editing process when everything comes together in a gestalt: the book emerges out of the letters, spaces, words and sentences; I can enjoy and appreciate it as a whole . . . and I know we are almost home.

In 1998, the field pulled me into systemic work, in the form of a 5-day training course, and have been busy with it ever since, guided mostly by Judith Hemming and Jan Jacob Stam.

I was born in London in 1950 of Scottish parents and now live in an intentional community, in Eindhoven, the Netherlands, with my wife, our 8-year-old daughter and our wiry Vizla. I've been working as an editor for about 10 years and as a systemic editor and systemic coach for about five years.

On any given day I try to touch base with, soul, poetry, nature and Manchester United.

James can be contacted via www.thelastword.eu

Want to read a bit further?

Hellinger, Bert, The Art of Helping. Groningen (Het Noorderlicht), 2004.

Kaat, Siebke and de Kroon, Anton, Systemic Consulting: The Organisation as a Living System. Groningen (Het Noorderlicht), 2013.

Stam, Jan Jacob, Wings for Change. Groningen (Het Noorderlicht), 2012.

Stam, Jan Jacob, Fields of Connection: The Practice of Organisational Constellations. Groningen (Het Noorderlicht), 2004.

Whittington, John, Systemic Coaching & Constellations. London (Kogan Page), 2012.

Systemic Books – inviting you

The platform for the best literature on systemic work you can find.

Systemic Books is an independent Publishing House focused on creating high quality content out of the broad range of books available. The books range from classic works to cutting edge works with new adaptations of the systemic way of thinking and working. This way, she aims to answer to the diversity in knowledge people have or need. From starter to experts on systemic thinking, everyone can enrich his knowledgde here.

Systemic Books aims to strengthen our understanding and appreciation of the systemic way of working. The systemic perspective is first a paradigm shift and then progresses past the challenges the world faces today.

We translate, edit and publish books. Great books about systemic thinking and working. We make use of all modern possibilities in publishing and printing to make these books available all over the world. The ownership always remains with the author. By doing this, we create the strongest and most vivid place for the books that is possible.

SystemicBooks is an international Publishing House founded in joint energy by Siets Bakker and Barbara Piper in 2016. When we met in 2015, their knowledge of and interest in the systemic perspective and our shared love for books, planted the seed for SystemicBooks. This initiative combines our knowledge in the publishing world and efforts to make systemic work available to a global audience.

www.systemicbooks.com

systemicbooks
inviting you

www.ingramcontent.com/pod-product-compliance
Lightning Source LLC
Chambersburg PA
CBHW070846310526
45793CB00012B/655